aiRevolution.tech

The ultimate database of AI-powered creative tools and resources

ARTIFICIAL INTELLIGENCE & THE CREATOR ECONOMY

150 ways creators can leverage AI to stand-out, stay competitive and make big money

All rights reserved. No portion of this book may be reproduced in any form without prior permission from the copyright owner of this book.

Copyright © 2023 AI Revolution Press

ARTIFICIAL INTELLIGENCE IS NOT AN ENEMY, IT'S A TOOL.

Creators who embrace artificial intelligence will become those who end-up on the top.

AI has become one of the most powerful tools in the world for creating wealth and improving the lives of millions of people.

From simple tasks to finding new and innovative ways to solve problems, AI is transforming the way that businesses and entrepreneurs are generating revenue. With the increasing availability of AI technologies, it has never been easier for creatives to leverage these powerful tools to improve their bottom line.

There are hundreds of ways that creatives can use AI to make money, including automating repetitive tasks such as image recognition and data analysis, as well as finding new and innovative solutions to challenges they face in their creative endeavors. AI can be used to create personalized recommendations for customers, automate the production of high-quality content, and even help artists and designers find new and exciting ways to express their creativity.

Despite the many benefits of AI, many creatives are still hesitant to embrace these technologies. They may worry that AI will replace their jobs or that it will be too complex to learn and use. However, with the increasing availability of AI tools and resources, **it has never been easier for creatives to start using AI to improve their bottom line.** Whether you are a freelance designer, a small business owner, or an established artist, there is an AI solution that can help you achieve your goals and create wealth for yourself and your community.

FIVE REASONS CREATORS NEED TO START LEVERAGING ARTIFICIAL INTELLIGENCE, NOW.

Increased Efficiency

AI can help creatives automate routine and repetitive tasks, freeing up time for more important and creative work. For example, AI can be used to automate the editing process in film or the selection process in graphic design. This increased efficiency can lead to higher productivity and improved bottom lines for creative businesses.

Competitive Advantage

AI is becoming increasingly common in the creative industries, and those who do not adopt these technologies risk being left behind. By leveraging AI, creatives can gain a competitive advantage by being able to work faster, smarter, and more efficiently than their competition.

New Revenue Streams

AI has the potential to open up new revenue streams for creatives. For example, AI can be used to create personalized recommendations for customers, or to generate new and innovative content that can be monetized. These new revenue streams can provide a significant boost to the bottom line of creative businesses."

Improved Customer Experience

AI can be used to create a more personalized and engaging experience for customers. AI can be used to analyze customer data and preferences, and then provide customized recommendations or create personalized content based on that information. This can lead to increased customer satisfaction, loyalty, and revenue for creative businesses.

Access to Cutting-Edge Technologies

AI is a rapidly evolving field, and by embracing these technologies, creatives can access the latest and most advanced tools and techniques. This can provide a significant advantage in terms of staying ahead of the competition and staying on the cutting edge of the creative industries. In conclusion, it is clear that the use of AI in the creative industries is becoming increasingly important, and that those who do not embrace these technologies risk falling behind.

Whether you are a small business owner, a freelancer, or an established creative, the benefits of using AI are clear and undeniable. By leveraging AI, you can improve your workflow, increase your revenue, and stay ahead of the competition.

THE FOLLOWING PAGES LIST 150 WAYS YOU SHOULD BE LEVERAGING AI AS A CREATOR.

In all honesty, we could have created a list of 150,000 ways, as the possibilities are almost endless. **Consider this a jumping-off point to help you see what is possible, and where you can start to leverage this technology. The sky is the limit!**

If you are liking this book, please do us a huge favor and consider reviewing it on Amazon or Goodreads. We want to provide content that is valuable to you, in understanding how you can leverage AI to make money and create ease in your life. Thank you so much!

50 CREATOR FUNCTIONS THAT AI CAN ELEVATE AND ENHANCE.

From enhancing virtual and augmented reality experiences to automating graphic design and social media management, the possibilities for using AI in creative industries are vast and varied. Other applications include speech recognition for voice-controlled interfaces, sentiment analysis for improved customer service, recommendation systems for personalized content curation, and computer vision for advanced image and video analysis.

These are just a few examples of the 50 ways that creators can leverage AI to streamline processes, increase efficiency, and unlock new revenue streams. With the ongoing advancements in AI technology, the potential applications are endless, offering endless opportunities for creativity and innovation in the world of creation.

1.
CONTENT CREATION

AI can generate new and original content that can be monetized.

2.
CONTENT OPTIMIZATION

AI can analyze content to make suggestions for improvement, increasing its earning potential.

3.
ADVERTISING

AI can identify target audiences and optimize ad placements to increase monetization.

4.
AFFILIATE MARKETING

AI can identify products and services that align with content, increasing earnings through affiliate marketing.

5.
CONTENT PROMOTION

AI can analyze audience data to optimize content promotion strategies, reaching more potential customers and increasing monetization.

6.
E-COMMERCE

AI can power chatbots and virtual assistants to help with sales and customer service, improving the overall shopping experience for customers and boosting revenue.

7.
ROYALTIES AND LICENSING

AI can automate the tracking and distribution of royalties and licensing fees, streamlining the process and increasing revenue.

8.
SUBSCRIPTION MEMBERSHIP MANAGEMENT

AI can assist with managing subscribers and members, helping creators to grow their audience and revenue.

9.
CROWDFUNDING

AI can analyze audience data to determine the best crowdfunding strategies, increasing the chances of a successful campaign and earning potential.

10. BUSINESS AUTOMATION

AI can help streamline creator's business processes, reducing operational costs, and freeing up time for monetizing activities.

11.
AUDIENCE ANALYSIS

AI can help creators understand their audience and create content that appeals to them, resulting in increased engagement and revenue.

12.
COPYRIGHT PROTECTION

AI can assist with detecting and preventing copyright infringement, protecting creators' work and income.

13.
SALES PREDICTIONS

AI can help predict demand for creators' products and services, enabling them to make informed decisions about pricing and production.

14.
BRAND PROTECTION

AI can assist with monitoring and removing counterfeit products, protecting creators' brand reputation and income.

15.
PRODUCT RECOS

AI can make product recommendations by analyzing consumer behavior and predicting which products will be most appealing to their target audience.

16.
SUBSCRIPTION SERVICES

AI can personalize content and recommend new offerings based on subscriber preferences and behavior.

17. E-COMMERCE INTEGRATION

AI can help by by optimizing product recommendations, predicting consumer behavior, and streamlining the checkout process for a seamless shopping experience.

18.
MONETIZATION THROUGH ADVERTISEMENTS

AI can optimize ad content, placement and targeting, increasing the effectiveness and profitability of ads.

19.
PREMIUM CONTENT OFFERINGS

AI can identify and create high-value content and target those who are more likely to subscribe to premium content.

20.
VIRTUAL EVENTS AND EXPERIENCES

AI can create personalized experiences, automate event management tasks, and optimize virtual environments for engagement and monetization.

21.
PRODUCT CREATION & SALE

AI can forecast consumer preferences and market trends, streamlining production processes, and optimizing sales and marketing strategies.

22.
STREAMLINE WORKFLOW

AI can automate repetitive tasks, optimize processes, and free up time for higher-value creative and strategic activities.

23.
SEARCH ENGINE OPTIMIZATION

AI can analyze web traffic, keywords, and content, to provide recommendations for optimization and improved visibility and discoverability of content on search engines.

24.
BRAND SPONSORSHIPS

AI can seek brand sponsorships by analyzing audience behavior and preferences, matching with relevant brands, and streamlining communication and negotiation processes.

25.
PREDICTIVE MARKET ANALYSIS

AI can analyze data on consumer behavior, market trends, and competitor activity to make informed predictions about future market conditions and guide strategic decision-making.

26.
ARTICLE WRITING

AI can suggest topic ideas, generate outlines, and even write parts of articles based on data analysis and language models, saving time and improving content quality.

27.
STORYTELLING

AI can suggest story arcs, character development, and plot points based on data analysis and language models, allowing for more effective storytelling.

28.
BRAND MESSAGING

AI can analyze consumer behavior, market trends, and competitor activity to create effective and consistent messaging that resonates with their target audience.

29.
VOICEOVER SCRIPTS

AI can generate suggestions for script content and pacing based on data analysis and language models, enabling more efficient and effective voice over production.

30.
YOUTUBE THUMBNAILS

AI can generate thumbnail options based on audience behavior, video content, and brand consistency, improving the click-through rate and overall performance of videos.

31.
VISUAL DESIGN

AI can create options for visual content based on data analysis and deep learning models, providing new and innovative ideas for design projects.

32.
BRAND NAMES

AI can make suggestions based on analysis of popular and effective brand names, streamlining the naming process for businesses and products.

33.
SOCIAL MEDIA CAPTIONS

AI can help write captions based on data analysis of other popular captions, saving time and improving the engagement of social media posts.

34.
SOCIAL MEDIA BIOS

AI can write an effective and catchy social media bio that will resonate with your audience.

35.
VOICE OVERS

AI can create voice overs using human voices by using speech synthesis technology to generate a human-like voice based on deep learning models trained on real human speech.

36.
VIRTUAL ASSISTANT

AI can be your virtual assistant by performing tasks and answering questions through natural language processing and machine learning, freeing up time and increasing productivity.

37.
BRAINSTORMING

AI can expand the pool of ideas and encourage creative thinking by providing creative options.

38.
KEYWORD SUGGESTIONS

AI can generate keywords by analyzing data on search trends and patterns, providing relevant keywords to improve search visibility and reach.

39.
CONTENT CALENDAR

AI can create a content schedule by using algorithms to predict audience engagement and suggest optimal times for content publication, improving visibility and audience reach.

40.
FAQS

AI can automate the process of answering common questions, providing quick and accurate responses, reducing the workload for customer support teams, and improving audience satisfaction.

41.
COURSES

AI can write outlines for courses by analyzing and summarizing existing material, generating structured outlines, and recommending additional resources to enhance the curriculum.

42.
LOGO DEVELOPMENT

AI can create logo options for you for your own brand or product, or to sell to customers or clients.

43.
PHOTO MOCKUPS

AI can produce photo quality renditions of just about anything you can dream up.

44.
HEADLINES

AI can analyze headlines to capitalize on trends and popular culture to create content that is both relevant and captivating.

45.
EXPAND YOUR REACH

AI can translate your content to any language, helping you to reach markets across the globe.

46.
AUTO CAPTIONS

AI can recognize vocal patterns to create accurate captions from audio, to support those who prefer or need captions.

47.
EMAIL RESPONSES

AI can answer emails to save time and shorten response time.

48.
ANALYTICS

AI can generate analytics and reports that can help inform creative and business decisions.

49.
PRODUCT DESCRIPTIONS

AI can help to create product descriptions based on analysis and research, to talk specifically to the target market the product is being sold to.

50.
IMPROVED WRITING

AI can polish your writing by not only checking spelling and grammar, but by adding character and tone.

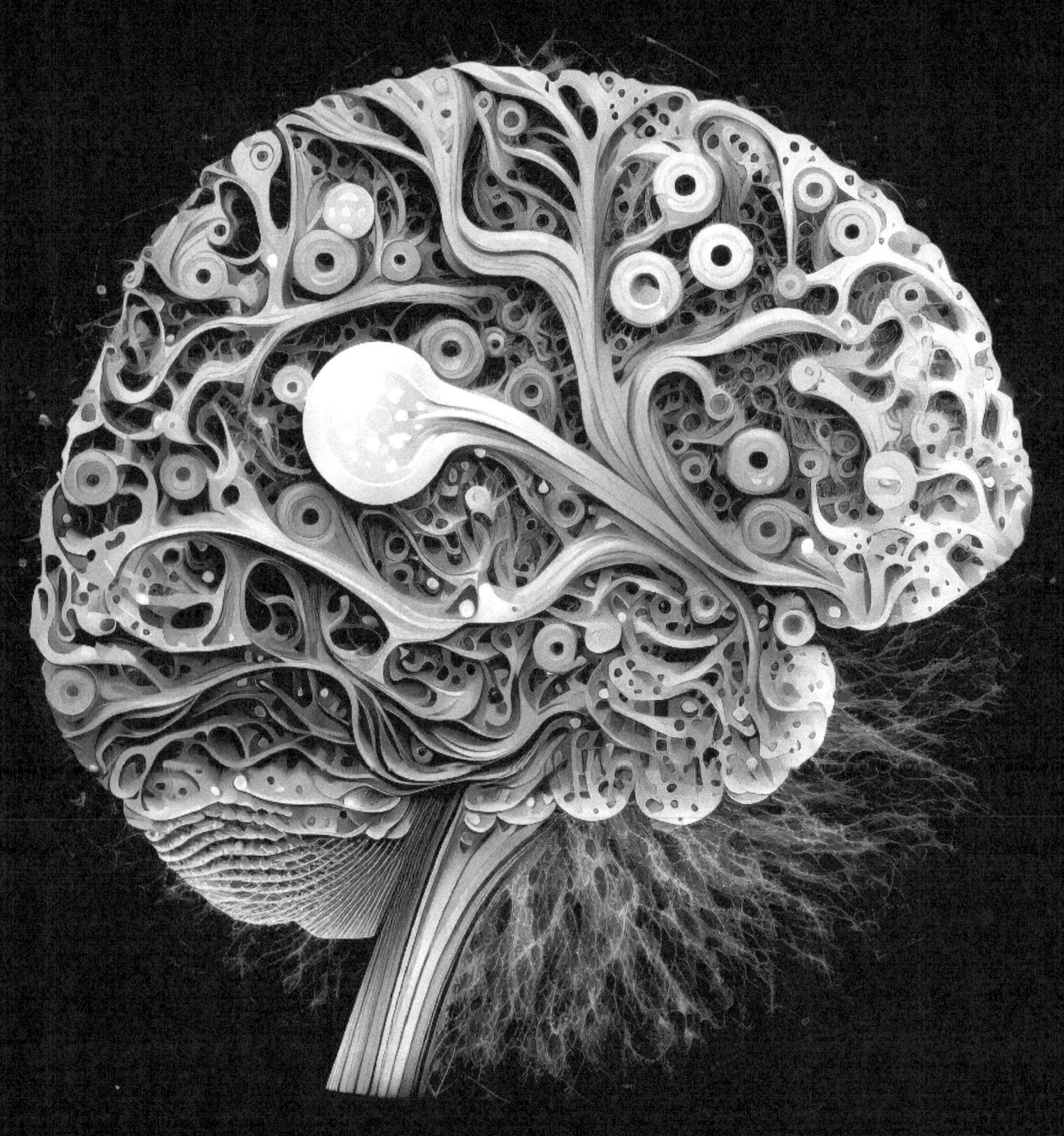

100 ADDITIONAL AI APPLICATIONS AND IDEAS THAT CREATORS CAN LEVERAGE AS OPPORTUNITIES

The potential uses of AI in the creative industries are virtually limitless, and as the technology continues to evolve, so too will the ways in which creators can leverage it to improve their work and grow their businesses.

There are many specific and practical ways that creators can use AI to improve their workflow and increase their revenue. For example, graphic designers can leverage AI for automatic image recognition and color correction, while filmmakers can use AI-powered tools for special effects and computer-generated imagery. Musicians can utilize AI for composing and producing new tracks, and writers can use AI for content generation and editing. In addition, AI can be used in the creative process to generate new ideas, analyze data to inform creative decisions, and automate routine tasks to free up time for more important tasks.

The following pages list one-hundred additional ideas for leveraging AI as a creator.

51. Writing prompts
52. Generating copy for websites
53. Writing news reports
54. Podcasts scripts
55. Generating jokes and humor
56. Providing trivia and information
57. Summarizing articles and documents
58. Writing resumes and cover letters
59. Responding to customer reviews
60. Writing personal letters and emails
61. Writing creative fiction and poetry
62. Creating unique usernames
63. Writing song lyrics
64. Improving public speaking
65. Generating data visualizations
66. Writing legal documents
67. Generating product and service comparisons
68. Improving public relations with press releases
69. Writing persuasive and argumentative essays
70. Creating and solving puzzles and riddles
71. Writing and evaluating research papers
72. Improving accessibility for visually impaired with alt text
73. Writing and designing newsletters
74. Writing business plans and proposals
75. Generating ideas for podcasts and webinars

76. Answering customer service inquiries
77. Writing resumes and job applications
78. Improving mental health with meditations and affirmations
79. Writing code snippets and tutorials
80. Providing coding and technical support
81. Generating design concepts and mockups
82. Providing real-time language translation
83. Writing and designing surveys and questionnaires
84. Improving communication skills with conversation tips
85. Writing grant proposals
86. Providing travel advice and recommendations
87. Generating home and garden ideas
88. Writing and publishing e-books
89. Relationship advice
90. Generating and organizing project plans and timelines
91. Writing creative non-fiction and memoirs
92. Providing health and wellness tips
93. Generating fashion and beauty ideas
94. Writing educational resources and study guides
95. Providing education and learning resources
96. Writing and delivering inspiring speeches
97. Writing and editing resumes and LinkedIn profiles
98. Providing dating and relationship advice
99. Personal finance tips and advice
100. Generating gift ideas for special occasions

101. Writing and publishing a cookbook
102. Providing exercise and fitness advice
103. Scheduling and organization tips
104. Writing and publishing a children's books
105. Poetry creation
106. Songwriting
107. Book writing
108. Cover letter writing
109. Business plan writing
110. Marketing plan writing
111. Menu development
112. Sales pitch writing
113. Presentation scripts
114. How-to guides
115. Instructional writing
116. Chatbot responses
117. Customer service scripts
118. Email response templates
119. Tweets
120. Memes
121. GIFs
122. Comics
123. Career advice
124. Worksheets
125. Study guides

126. Flashcards
127. Teaching aids
128. Lesson plans
129. Interactive activities
130. Webinars
131. Radio scripts
132. Audio books
133. Animation scripts
134. Music bed recommendations
135. Interactive stories
136. Game scripts
137. Game design documents and assets
138. Level design
139. World building
140. Character creation
141. Concept art
142. Storyboarding
143. 3D modeling
144. Motion graphics
145. Visual effects
146. Music composition
147. Sound design
148. Live performance scripts
149. Automated DJ sets
150. Creator & author bios

AS A CREATIVE, YOU ARE IMPROVING YOUR WORK AND STANDING OUT IN YOUR FIELD.

Now get started! By using artificial intelligence, you can unlock new levels of creativity and efficiency in your work. By embracing AI, you can stay ahead of the curve and push the boundaries of what's possible in your field.

CREATORS SUPPORT CREATORS.

If you liked this book, please do us a huge favor and consider reviewing it on Amazon or Goodreads. We want to provide content that is valuable to you, and your feedback is invaluable.

Thank you so much!

www.ingramcontent.com/pod-product-compliance
Lightning Source LLC
Chambersburg PA
CBHW080524220526
45465CB00006B/2593